The United States Capitol

By Charles River Editors

Martin Falbisoner's picture of the Capitol

About Charles River Editors

Charles River Editors provides superior editing and original writing services across the digital publishing industry, with the expertise to create digital content for publishers across a vast range of subject matter. In addition to providing original digital content for third party publishers, we also republish civilization's greatest literary works, bringing them to new generations of readers via ebooks.

Sign up here to receive updates about free books as we publish them, and visit Our Kindle Author Page to browse today's free promotions and our most recently published Kindle titles.

Introduction

Martin Falbisoner's picture of the Capitol

The Capitol Building

"The cornerstone was laid by Washington in 1793; the terrace was finished nearly a hundred years later, in 1891; and yet the Capitol will never be complete while the nation lasts. The impress of each succeeding generation will be found upon its walls, marking the intellectual, artistic and governmental advancement of the age. The great pile is national, American, human. On its walls is written the nation's history. Its corridors resound to the footsteps of her living heroes and sages; its every stone echoes the departed voices of her greatest dead." – George Hazelton

For over two centuries, the capital of America has been located in Washington, D.C., and among all the iconic landmarks and monuments associated with the city, nothing is as conspicuous as the Capitol, the magnificent building that houses Congress and sits on Capitol Hill at the epicenter of the city. At the same time, even though the Capitol is now one of the most recognizable buildings in the world, the image everyone is familiar with took decades to achieve, and its grand scope belies its rather chaotic history. In fact, the Capitol was partially burned by the British during the War of 1812, and its now famous dome was still under construction while the nation fought itself during the Civil War. Moreover, it's easy to forget that the expansion of the country resulted in the addition of new Congressmen, requiring the expansion of the Capitol as the seat of the legislative branch.

The Capitol truly remained a work in progress until the end of the 19th century, and until recently, it was possible to drive cars nearly to the steps leading up to the building. That changed in the wake of the attacks of September 11, 2001, and since then, much has been done to secure the grounds, including extending the property line outward, placing permanent barriers around the building, and adding a visitor center through which tourists can be routed. Even in this new era, however, it is easy for visitors in the Capitol to sense the history around every corner; as Kansas Congressman Kevin Yoder once put it, "Certainly in the Capitol you do get moments were you sort of take a deep breath and think of all the historic figures who have been in that building, like Abraham Lincoln, who have stood right in those same rooms to make the landmark decisions."

The history of the Capitol also serves as a reminder that the building, like the nation, both shapes and is shaped by history. There are still singed walls from the War of 1812 under the marble façade, and microscopic examination could no doubt find cracks from the vibration of distant cannon fire during the Civil War. Of course, there is no way to calculate the wear and tear caused by the millions of feet that trudge through the Capitol's sacred halls each year, but through it all, the Capitol has managed to endure, just like the nation it represents.

The United States Capitol Building: The History and Legacy of the Seat of Congress looks at the winding history of the building and how it has changed over time. Along with pictures of important people, places, and events, you will learn about the Capitol like never before, in no time at all.

The United States Capitol Building: The History and Legacy of the Seat of Congress
About Charles River Editors
Introduction
- Chapter 1: In a Perfect Union
- Chapter 2: Grandeur, Simplicity and Beauty
- Chapter 3: In the Old North Wing
- Chapter 4: The Whole Structure Was Soon in Flames
- Chapter 5: Four Historical Paintings
- Chapter 6: Great Difficulty
- Chapter 7: An Unfinished Appearance
- Bibliography

Chapter 1: In a Perfect Union

"Wise, however, as he was in the choice of the site, it is noticeable that Washington selected it as near as possible, under the act, to his own home at Mount Vernon; and in the amendment of March 3, 1791, his hand can be plainly seen. This, while it still limited the erection of the public buildings to the Maryland side of the Potomac, allowed a portion of the district to be located below the Eastern Branch and above the mouth of Hunting Creek, so as to include a convenient part of the Branch and the town of Alexandria. The great man watched with anxiety over the founding of the Federal City, which was to bear his name, and with eagerness hastened the erection of its government buildings, as if with them to anchor public interest to the spot on which his hopes raised a city whose destiny was to be kindred to the growth and grandeur of a nation of the people. Himself a Federalist, he doubtless foresaw as well, in this one Capitol, an ultimate recognition of Federal supremacy, and, in a perfect union, respectful alike to State and nation, a government strong enough to protect itself and its every citizen." – George Cochrane Hazelton, *The National Capitol: Its Architecture, Art and History*

On July 1, 1790, almost 14 years to the day after declaring to Britain and all the world that America would be an independent nation, the newly formed United States Congress passed the Residence Act, which authorized a committee of their peers to find the new nation a permanent capital city. The sixth clause stated emphatically, "AND BE IT ENACTED, That on the said first Monday in December in the year one thousand eight hundred the seat of the government of the United States shall by virtue of this Act be transferred to the district and place aforesaid; and all Offices attached to the said seat of government shall accordingly be removed thereto by their respective holders, and shall after the said day cease to be exercised elsewhere; and that the necessary expense of such removal shall be defrayed out of the duties on imports and tonnage; of which a sufficient sum is hereby appropriated."

As such, the three men appointed as Commissioners by President George Washington - Thomas Johnson, D. D. Stuart and Daniel Carroll - had a little over 10 years to find land, choose plans, hire builders and erect a new city for the young government to move to. People today may be accustomed to seeing skyscrapers built in a matter of a few years, but in 1790, the most sophisticated building tools workers had to use were a block and tackle. Therefore, the Commissioners had their work cut out for them.

The first step was to find the land, which proved relatively easy when Virginia and Maryland willingly donated 10 acres of prime swampland along the Potomac to federal use. Next, the men had to find someone capable of not just designing a building but an entire city, and they found such a man in Pierre L'Enfant, who declared enthusiastically, "No nation had ever before the opportunity offered them of deliberately deciding on the spot where their Capital City should be fixed, or of combining every necessary consideration in the choice of situation, and although the means now within the power of the Country are not such as to pursue the design to any great extent, it will be obvious that the plan should be drawn on such a scale as to leave room for that aggrandizement and embellishment which the increase of the wealth of the nation will permit it to pursue at any period however remote."

L'Enfant

Though modern commuters caught in Washington D.C.'s traffic during rush hour may curse his name, L'Enfant's plans were well-suited for the people and conveyances of his time. He explained, "Having determined some principal points to which I wished to make others subordinate, I made the distribution regular with every street at right angles, North and South, east and west, and afterwards opened some in different directions, as avenues to and from every principal place, wishing thereby not merely to contract with the general regularity, nor to afford a greater variety of seats with pleasant prospects, which will be obtained from the advantageous ground over which these avenues are chiefly directed, but principally to connect each part of the city, if I may so express it, by making the real distance less from place to place, by giving to them a reciprocity of sight and by making them thus seemingly connected, promote a rapid settlement over the whole extent."

At the center of L'Enfant's plans lay the Federal House, the home of the legislative branch of the government. Of this all important building he wrote, "After much minutial search for an eligible situation, prompted I may say from a fear of being prejudiced in favor of a first opinion I could discover no one so advantageously to greet the congressional building as is that on the west end of Jenkins heights which stand as a pedestal waiting for a monument, and I am

confident, were all the wood cleared from the ground no situation could stand in competition with this, some might perhaps require less labor to be rendered agreeable but after all assistance of arts none ever would be made so grand and all other would appear but of secondary nature.
… The grand avenue connecting both the palace and the Federal House will be most magnificent and most convenient, the streets running west of the upper square of the Federal House and which terminate in an easy slope on the canal through the Tiber [river] which it will overlook for the space of about two miles will be beautiful above what may be imagined — those other streets parallel to that canal, those crossing over it and which are as many avenues to the grand walk from the water cascade under the Federal House to the President park and dependently extending to the bank of the Potomac."

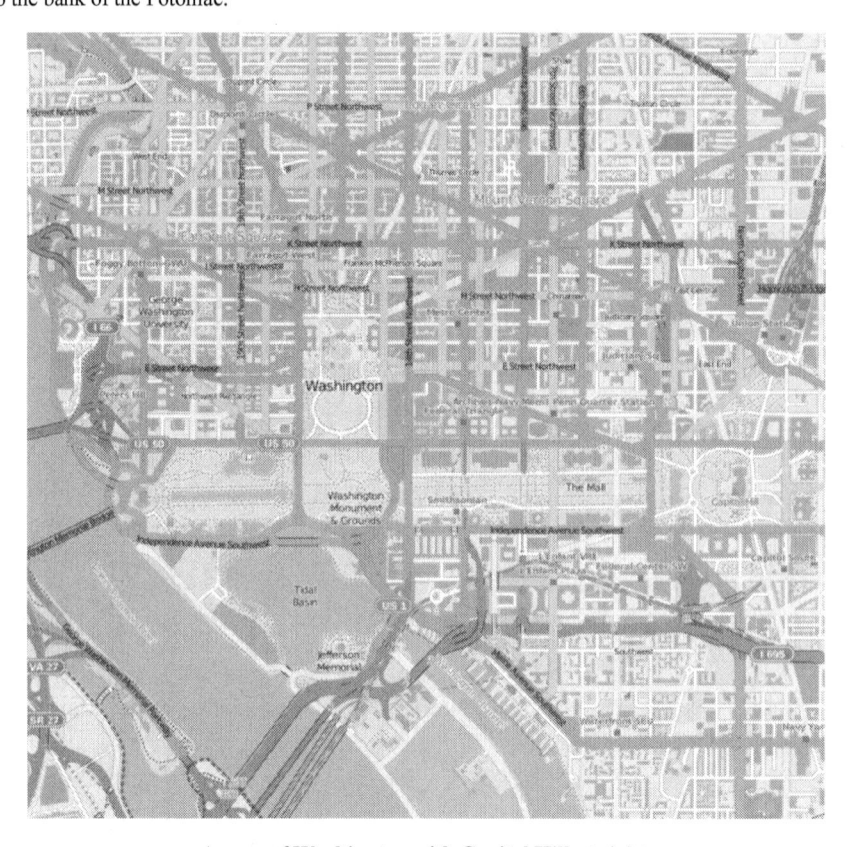

A map of Washington with Capitol Hill at right

While L'Enfant referred to it as the Federal House, a Founding Father familiar with architecture, Thomas Jefferson, ultimately insisted that the home of the legislative branch be known as the Capitol instead of Congress or Federal House. The groundbreaking was held during the first week of October in 1791, and fittingly, the ground for both the White House and the Capitol Building were broken on the same day. L'Enfant ordered, "The planting of the wall of the terrace fronting from Congress House towards the President's Palace and for the gradual assent to the Federal Square which will be made of earth from the foundation."

Supervising both projects, L'Enfant hired 150 workers to begin digging the foundations for both buildings, and it was also recorded that "on the 16th day of November, 1791, L'Enfant on behalf of the Public hath rented from John Gibson for ten years to commence on the 10th day of next month, all quarries of freestone on the land of Aquaia Creek at a yearly rental of Twenty pounds current money to be paid to the said John Gibson on the first day of December in every year."

The men worked hard through the winter, and by spring of 1792, the Commissioners running the operations were ready to authorize construction to begin on the new Capitol.

The Capitol Building used in New York City

Congress Hall, the Capitol Building used in Philadelphia

Depiction of the interior of Congress Hall, the Capitol Building used in Philadelphia

Chapter 2: Grandeur, Simplicity and Beauty

"Of the sixteen plans which, in answer to this advertisement, are said to have been submitted by architects, draftsmen and others throughout the country, many persons, including Thomas Jefferson, then Secretary of State, favored those of Stephen Hallet, a French architect, who had established himself in Philadelphia just prior to the Revolution. Hallet visited the city of Washington by invitation in the summer of 1792, in order to examine the site chosen for the Capitol and better to perfect his designs. These would undoubtedly have been accepted, had not William Thornton, an English physician by education, but an amateur draftsman by taste, and the designer of the Philadelphia Library, then brought to the President's attention through Trumbull, the artist, a different conception of a building designed for the meetings of Congress. Washington, at the sight of Thornton's drawings, became enthusiastic over 'the grandeur, simplicity, and beauty of the exterior; the propriety with which the apartments are distributed, and economy in the whole mass of the structure.'" – George Cochrane Hazelton, *The National Capitol: Its Architecture, Art and History*

While L'Enfant earned himself a place in history through his design of the city's layout, Washington considered his building designs too grand for the new republic and fired him in February 1792. Alongside Jefferson, he convinced the government to sponsor a design contest open to anyone wishing to design the Capitol, and thus, the following advertisement was run:

"WASHINGTON IN THE TERRITORY OF COLUMBIA

"A premium of a lot in this city to be designated by impartial judges, and live hundred dollars, or a medal of that value at the option of the party, will be given by the Commissioners of the Federal Buildings to the person who before the 15th of July, 1792, shall produce to them the most approved plan for a Capitol to be erected in this city ; and two hundred and fifty dollars, or a medal, to the plan deemed next in merit to the one they shall adopt. The building to be of brick, and to contain the following apartments to wit: a conference-room and a room for the Representatives, sufficient to accommodate three hundred persons each; a lobby or ante-room to the latter; a Senate room of twelve hundred square feet area; an ante-chamber; twelve rooms of six hundred square feet each for Committee rooms and clerks' offices. It will be a recommendation of any plan if the central part of it may be detached and erected for the present with the appearance of a complete whole, and be capable of admitting the additional parts in future, if they shall be wanted. Drawings will be expected of the ground plots, elevations of each front, and sections through the building in such directions as may be necessary to explain the internal structure; and an estimate of the cubic feet of brick work composing the whole mass to the walls."

Ultimately, none of the plans offered before the deadline impressed the Commission, which is why Dr. William Thornton, a physician and self-trained architect, was allowed to submit his entry on January 31, 1793. His entry would go on to win the competition, and in reference to his training and philosophy regarding architectural design, Thornton later wrote, "I travelled in many parts of Europe, and saw several of the masterpieces of the ancients. I have studied the works of the best masters, and my long attention to drawing and painting would enable me to form some judgment of the difference of proportions. An acquaintance with some of the grandest of the ancient structures, a knowledge of the orders of Architecture, and also of the genuine effects of proportion furnish the requisites of the great outlines of composition. The minutiae are attainable by a more attentive study of what is necessary to the execution of such works, and the whole must be subservient to the conveniences required. Architecture embraces many subordinate studies, and it must be admitted is a profession which requires great talents, great taste, great memory."

Thornton

James Diamond's design for the Capitol Building, one of the submissions rejected by the commission

Washington immediately preferred Thornton's plans, writing, "Doctor Thornton has also given me a view of his. These last came forward under some very advantageous circumstances. — The grandeur, simplicity, and beauty of the exterior ; the propriety with which the apartments are distributed, and economy in the whole mass of the structure will I doubt not give it a preference in your eyes, as it has done in mine, and those of several others whom I have consulted, and who are deemed men of skill in architecture. I have therefore thought it better to give the Doctor time to finish his plan and for this purpose to delay 'till your next meeting a final decision."

The Commission accepted Thornton's plans but appointed the second runner up, Stephen Hallet, to review them and supervise the construction. It instructed him in a letter on February 13, 1793, "The plan you first offered for a Capitol appeared to us to have a great share of merit, none met with our entire approbation. Yours approaching the nearest to the leading ideas of the President and Commissioners. . . . Our opinion has preferred Doctor Thornton's and we expect the President will confirm our choice. Neither the Doctor or yourself can command the prize under the strict terms of our advertisement, but the public has been benefitted by the emulation excited and the end having been answered we shall give the reward of 500 dollars and a lot to Dr.

Thornton. You certainly rank next and because your application has been exited by particular request, we have resolved to place you on the same footing as near as may be, that is to allow compensation for everything to this time, 100 £ being the value of a Lot and 500 Dollars."

Over the next several months, Hallet insisted that significant changes be made to Thornton's design based on his experience as a working architect, experience Thornton didn't have. Then, in July 1793, Washington sat down with both men, as well as James Hoban (who was designing the President's House) and Colonel Williams (whom Thornton had chosen as the builder for the project) to work out any differences in design. Washington subsequently wrote, "After a candid discussion, it was found that the objections stated, were considered as valid by both the persons chosen by Doctor Thornton as practical Architects and competent judges of things of this kind. . . . The plan produced by Mr. Hallet although preserving the original plan of Doctor Thornton, and such as might, upon the whole, be considered as his plan, was free from those objections, and was pronounced by the gentleman on the part of Doctor Thornton, as the one which they, as practical Architects would choose to execute. Besides which, you will see, that, in the opinion of those gentlemen, the plan executed according to Mr. Hallet's ideas would not cost more than one half of what it would if executed according to Doctor Thornton's. After these opinions, there could remain no hesitation how to decide; and Mr. Hoban was accordingly informed that the foundation would be begun upon the plan exhibited by Mr. Hallet, leaving the recess in the east front open for further consideration. It seems to be the wish that the portico of the east front, which was in Doctor Thornton's original plan, should be preserved in this of Mr. Hallet's. The recess which Mr. Hallet proposes in that front, strikes everyone who has viewed the plan, unpleasantly, as the space between the two wings or projections, is too contracted to give it the noble appearance of the buildings of which it is an imitation; and it has been intimated that the reason of his proposing the recess instead of a portico, is to take it in one essential feature different from Doctor Thornton's plan. But whether the portico or the recess should be finally concluded upon will make no difference in the commencement of the foundations of the building, except in that particular part — and Mr. Hallet is directed to make such sketches of the Portico, before the work will be affected by it, as will show the advantage or disadvantage thereof. The ostensible objection of Mr. Hallet to the adoption of Doctor Thornton's east front is principally the depreciation of light and air, in a degree, to the apartments designed for the Senate and Representatives."

Hoban

A few months later, the cornerstone for the Capitol was laid with as much pomp and fanfare as the Freemasons of the area could muster. The ceremony concluded when the "Grand Master delivered the Commissioners, a large silver plaque with an inscription thereon, which the Commissioners ordered to be read, and was as follows: 'This southeast corner stone of the Capitol of the United States of America, in the city of Washington was laid on the 18th, day of September, 1793, in the eighteenth year of American Independence, in the first year of the second term of the Presidency of George Washington, whose virtues in the civil administration of his country have been as conspicuous and beneficial as his military valor and prudence have been useful in establishing her liberties'…The plate was then delivered to the President, who…descended into the cavasson trench, and deposed the plate, and laid on it the cornerstone of the Capitol of the United States of America — on which was deposed corn, wine, and oil; when the whole congregation joined in awful prayer."

For the next year, Hallet worked diligently under Hoban's supervision to see the project completed, but he made the ill-fated move of defying the Commission's wishes and changing the East Front of the building from the way Thornton had designed it to create a square courtyard in the front, on either side of which would be housed the two legislative bodies. Jefferson fired Hallet in November 1794, and the work then remained dormant for nearly a year until George Hadfield was hired to replace Hallet in October 1795.

In November 1795, after he had gone behind their backs to complain to Washington about their actions, one of the Commissioners wrote to Hallet, "Your letter of the 31st [of least month] by Mr. Hadfield has been received. I have since seen Mr. Hoban. I have had a good deal of conversation with both of them, in the presence of each other, with the plans before us. From the explanation of the former, it would seem…that now he means no change in the interior of the building, of the least importance; nor any elsewhere, that will occasion delay, or add to the expense but the contrary: while the exterior will, in his opinion, assume a better appearance, and the portico be found more convenient than on the present plan. As far as I understand the matter, the difference lies simply in discarding the basement, & adding an attic story, if the latter shall be found necessary ; but this (the attic) he thinks may be dispersed, in the manner he has explained it, without— and to add a dome over the open or circular area or lobby, which in my judgment is a most desirable thing, & what I always expected was part of the original design, until otherwise informed in my late visit to the city, if strength can be given to it & sufficient light obtained. … I have told him in decis[ive] terms, however, that if the plan on which you have been proceeding, is not capitally defective, I cannot after such changes, delays, and expenses as have been encountered already) consent to a departure from it, if either of these consequences is to be involved : but that if he can satisfy you of the contrary, in these points,— I should have no objection, as he conceives his character as an architect is in some measure at stake ... to the proposed change provided these things, as I have just observed, can be ascertained to your entire satisfaction. I added further as a matter of material moment, the short term for which he was engaged, & what might be the consequence of his quitting the building at the end thereof, — or compelling fresh perhaps exorbitant terms, if a new agreement was to be made. To this he replied, that he would not only promise, but bind himself to stick by the building until it was finished."

Hadfield continued to supervise the construction until May 1798. Discouraged by what had been accomplished, he resigned, but while the work on the Capitol was again halted, the work of the government had to go on, and the December 1800 deadline for moving the capital to

Washington had to be met. On May 15, 1800, John Adams issued the following order: "The President requests the several heads of Departments to take the most prudent and economical arrangements for the removal of the public offices, clerks, and papers, according to their own best judgment, as soon as may be convenient, in such manner that the public offices may be opened in the City of Washington, for the dispatch of business, by the 15th of June."

A dome design proposed by Hadfield

Chapter 3: In the Old North Wing

"Both branches were then sitting in the old North Wing, as that was all that was then completed, and truly their conveniences do not seem to have been of the best; for, four days after convening, Thomas Claxton was directed to erect a shelter over the fire-wood required by the two Houses so as to protect it from the weather. For the furnishing of the apartments themselves, the offices and the committee rooms, as well as for the expenses of the removal of the books, records and papers of Congress from Philadelphia, only $9,000 had been appropriated, to be expended under the supervision of the Secretaries of the four Executive Departments. These Secretaries at the same time were to see that the Commissioners prepared footways in suitable places and directions for the 'greater facility of communication between the various Departments and offices of the Government.'" – George Cochrane Hazelton, *The National Capitol: Its Architecture, Art and History*

A depiction of the Capitol Building in 1800

The legislators arriving in Washington in 1800 to begin their work were in for a grave disappointment; instead of a mighty domed building with two wings like the kind they had seen on the architectural plans circulated among them, they found only the North Wing was complete. In fact, according to architect Benjamin Latrobe, who would help make critical changes to the White House during James Madison's presidency, much of the Capitol remained incomplete well into the 19th century. He later wrote, "In the year 1803 . . . that part of the South Wing of the Capitol in which the House of Representatives then sat was in such a state as to require building from the very foundation ... In the year 1803, the foundations of the external walls were condemned and pulled down. The center building occupied by the House of Representatives remained standing, — because in the opinion of many, a further appropriation appeared at least doubtful. The difficulty of working in the narrow space round that building can scarcely be conceived, and as the House met in December, all our men were of course discharged before that time. In 1804 the session concluded in March, & then first could our works commence. Much time was lost in pulling down and removing the old building, and before any new work could be begun. However, the progress made that year was great, considering all the disadvantages we labored under . . . As I had distinguished the recess from the South Wing, the omission to appropriate for that part appeared to forbid its erection. But the plan of the building was necessarily such, that the whole area of the South Wing was repaired for the Hall of the House of Representatives. The external walls therefore could receive no support from internal walls: — The southwest walls had been built so solidly and were so strengthened in the angles by the stair cases of the galleries, that there could be no danger of their giving way to the pressure of the vaults, — but the north wall which, in relation to the whole building, is an internal wall, and the support of which depended upon the recess, had not been calculated to stand alone. It was therefore carried up one story, and no alteration of consequence could be made…. That the House has not been completed, has been simply owing to this, that its completion was impossible in itself. When the President of the United States did me the honor to entrust to me the charge of the buildings, I found the North Wing already constructed, and a commencement made in the erection of the South Wing.

Latrobe

While the Congressmen continued to meet in the North Wing, a wooded "South Wing" was hastily constructed, and when it was finished, it was became the temporary home of the House of Representatives. Latrobe then went on to offer a detailed description of the work done as of 1806 and scheduled for the immediate future: "The entrance to the South Wing from the ground or office story will be in the recess. That in the east front will be closed, it being intended for a window. It has been opened to the ground only for the convenience of the workmen. The outer door leads into a hall or vestibule. On the left hand is a door opening into a committee room. From the vestibule four steps lead up to the area of the staircase which is lighted from the sky, and gives light, to the entrance, to the octagon vestibule of the offices, and to the stairs. On the left hand the stairs lead up to the door of the hall of Representatives on the principal floor. The area of the staircase is connected with the vestibule of the offices, into which, on the left, a spiral staircase for the convenience of the persons coming from above to the offices, descends. A door immediately in front leads into a court which contains the pump, furnishes light to the deep part of the buildings, and contains various domestic conveniences. On the right is the entrance to the center of the building, which will be the principal and public access to the Capitol. On the left hand of the octagon vestibule is the access to the offices, by the general passage or corridor. Immediately on entering the corridor and descending a few steps is a passage to a committee room on the right. The arched doors on each hand lead to deposits of fuel, and to the stoves which warm the hall above. This passage is crossed by a corridor running east and west. Immediately in front is the office of the clerk of the House. The center of the office is open for those who have business in it, — in each angle is a private office for the engrossing clerks, and around are six spacious vaults for the records of the House."

Having given readers a careful description of the larger rooms, he continued, "Returning into the corridor and proceeding to the west, you enter an antechamber, in which those who have business with the committees must wait. To the right are a small, and a large committee room, and to the left another of convenient size. The large committee room is accessible separately from the corridor. The east end of the corridor leads into another antechamber, which on the left communicates with two committee rooms, the largest of which opens also into the vestibule of the entrance. On the right is the room appropriated to the use of the President of the United States, whenever he shall come to the House. On the south front of the building near each end, are the doors of the gallery, which at present have the appearance of windows, but which will soon be cut down to the level of the other doors. Each door leads into a small lobby, from which a spiral staircase ascends to the gallery. These doors are so far distant from the entrance of the members to the House, that the inconvenience generally experienced by having only one entrance will be avoided. The principal access to the hall of Representatives will be — when the Capitol shall be finished, — from the center of the building, through the small circular vestibule. But the most usual entrance will always be from the basement story, & by the stairs in the recess. These stairs land at the door of the Legislative Hall on one side, as do the spiral stairs of the offices on the other. On entering the great door of the hall, the lobby of the House extends on both sides, and is separated from the area of the House by the basement wall upon which the columns of the House are erected. The bar of the House is the opening of this wall: opposite to it on the other side will be the Speaker's chair."

One of the things that Latrobe was most critical of was the building's acoustics: "The lobby of the House is so separated from it, that those who retire to it cannot see, and probably will not distinctly hear, what is going forward in it. This arrangement has been made with the approbation of the President of the United States, and also under the advice of the Speakers of the two houses. The construction of the Hall of Representatives was imposed by the general plan of the work. Whether it will be a room, in which to hear & to speak will be easy, can only be determined by actual experiment. All that the knowledge to which I can pretend, could do, has been done to make it so, by surrounding the area with a plain surface, and raising the columns above the heads of the speakers, and I believe this attempt will be successful. Rooms encumbered with many columns and projecting cornices are not well adapted to the ease of hearing and speaking. Of this truth the Chamber of the Senate is perhaps the most striking proof that can be adduced. That it will be a splendid room, — probably the most splendid Legislative Hall that has ever been erected, — is certain: & it will also be extremely convenient in its arrangement, and remarkably warm in winter and cool in summer. The whole of the wing excepting the Legislative Hall is vaulted. It was originally intended that this dome should also be turned in bricks, and the construction is such that it may at any time, should the present dome of timber decay, be covered with a brick or stone dome. On the ground floor of the North Wing, including lobbies and stairs, are 12 apartments, — in the south are 22 apartments, lobbies & stairs, & il depots of records, & fuel cellars of cheaper construction; in all 33."

The South Wing was finally finished in 1811, but there was no building to join the two wings, only a covered wooden sidewalk. As fate would have it, both wings would be burned nearly to the ground before the main structure could be completed.

The Old Senate Chamber, which was used from 1810-1859

An 1822 depiction of the Old Hall of the House of Representatives, which later became National Statuary Hall

National Statuary Hall

Chapter 4: The Whole Structure Was Soon in Flames

"On reaching the Capitol, the enemy detailed a body of men to take possession of the building. Admiral Cockburn…impudently ascended the rostrum in the House of Representatives, sprang into the Speaker's chair in his muddy boots, and, calling his battle-stained troops to order in mock parliament, shouted derisively : 'Shall this harbor of Yankee Democracy be burned ? All for it will say. Aye!' An unanimous cry in the affirmative arose from the soldiers, and the order was cheerfully given. By means of rockets, tar barrels found in the neighborhood, broken furniture, heaps of books from the Library, and pictures…the whole structure was soon in flames. … Fortunately, the storm which had been threatening during the approach of the English, aided by a few patriotic hands, finally extinguished the flames. But too late! It is recorded as having had a velocity so great as to destroy many buildings and trees in the city, and as portending to the superstitious such dire calamity as the upheavals in Rome when Caesar fell." – George Cochrane Hazelton, *The National Capitol: Its Architecture, Art and History*

The close of 1812 saw the United States once again at war with England, and within a few years, it looked like the young country might lose this one. After over a year of mostly inconclusive fighting in 1813, the British invaders definitely had the upper hand in August 1814 when they landed in Baltimore harbor and began their march to the American capital. American troops fought valiantly but found themselves falling back again and again, and eventually they were pushed back to Washington and the Capitol Building. According to Charles Ingersall, one of the first historians to write about the war, "There, General Armstrong suggested throwing them into the two wings of that stone, strong building. But General Winder with warmth rejected the proposal. . . . Colonel Monroe [afterwards President] coincided with General Winder's opinion. The Capitol, he feared, might prove a cul-de-sac, from which there would be no escape ; the only safety was to rally on the heights beyond Georgetown. . . . Both at their first order to retreat toward the Capitol, and their last to retreat from it, and march beyond the city, insubordinate protests, oaths, tears, and bitter complaints broke forth."

General John Armstrong, Jr., who was also Secretary of War at the time

In August 1814, First Lady Dolley Madison wrote of the precarious situation for the First

Family during their last few days in the White House:

"Dear Sister

My husband left me yesterday morning to join Gen. Winder. He enquired anxiously whether I had courage, or firmness to remain in the President's house until his return, on the morrow, or succeeding day, and on my assurance that I had no fear but for him and the success of our army, he left me, beseeching me to take care of myself, and of the cabinet papers, public and private. I have since received two dispatches from him, written with a pencil; the last is alarming, because he desires I should be ready at a moment's warning to enter my carriage and leave the city; that the enemy seemed stronger than had been reported, and that it might happen that they would reach the city, with intention to destroy it. . . . . I am accordingly ready; I have pressed as many cabinet papers into trunks as to fill one carriage; our private property must be sacrificed, as it is impossible to procure wagons for its transportation. I am determined not to go myself until I see Mr. Madison safe, and he can accompany me, as I hear of much hostility towards him, ... Disaffection stalks around us. . . . My friends and acquaintances are all gone; Even Col. C with his hundred men, who were stationed as a guard in the enclosure . . . . French John (a faithful domestic,) with his usual activity and resolution, offers to spike the cannon at the gate, and to lay a train of powder which would blow up the British, should they enter the house. To the last proposition I positively object, without being able, however, to make him understand why all advantages in war may not be taken.

Wednesday morng., twelve o'clock. Since sunrise I have been turning my spyglass in every direction and watching with unwearied anxiety, hoping to discern the approach of my dear husband and his friends, but, alas, I can descry only groups of military wandering in all directions, as if there was a lack of arms, or of spirit to fight for their own firesides!

Three O'clock. Will you believe it, my Sister? We have had a battle or skirmish near Bladensburg, and I am still here within sound of the cannon! Mr. Madison comes not; may God protect him! Two messengers covered with dust, come to bid me fly; but I wait for him. . . . At this late hour a wagon has been procured, I have had it filled with the plate and most valuable portable articles belonging to the house; whether it will reach its destination; the Bank of Maryland, or fall into the hands of British soldiery, events must determine.

Our kind friend, Mr. Carroll, has come to hasten my departure, and is in a very bad humor with me because I insist on waiting until the large picture of Gen. Washington is secured, and it requires to be unscrewed from the wall. This process was found too tedious for these perilous moments; I have ordered the frame to be broken, and the canvass taken out it is done, and the precious portrait placed in the hands of two gentlemen of New York, for safe keeping. And now, dear sister, I must leave this house, or the retreating army will make me a prisoner in it, by filling up the road I am directed to take. When I shall again write you, or where I shall be tomorrow, I cannot tell!!"

Dolley did indeed get out of Washington in time, leaving dinner on the dining room table for her husband in case he should return in the night. However, she later learned that it was a British general who dined on her repast and then, after drinking a sarcastic toast to her with her own wine, proceeded to set fire to everything she had loved in her home.

James and Dolley Madison

Indeed, as soon as the British arrived in town, they set fire to all the major government buildings, including the Capitol, and though a rainstorm blew in later that night, there was still extensive damage. Reverend G.R. Gleig, who fought for the British, recalled the scene: "As soon as dawn appeared, the brigade moved from its bivouac on the common, and marched into the town. Proceeding along a narrow street, which was crossed at right angles by two or three of a 'similar description, we arrived at a large open space, surrounded on three sides by the rudiments of a square, and having its fourth imperfectly occupied by the ruins of the Senate-House. It is slightly raised above the level of the rest of the city, and is crossed by a paltry stream, called in true Yankee grandiloquence, the Tiber, as the hill itself is called the Capitol. Here the brigade halted, and piling their arms in two close columns, the men were permitted to lie down."

A depiction of the burned Capitol in 1814

Fortunately, the British did not occupy the town for long. On September 17, the Congress met in special session, where is was informed by President Madison: "The destruction of the Capitol, by the enemy, having made it necessary that other accommodations should be provided for the meeting of Congress, Chambers for the Senate and for the House of Representatives, with other requisite apartments, have been fitted up, under the direction of the Superintendent of the City, in the public building heretofore allotted for the Post and other public offices." Paul Jennings, one of Madison's most trusted slaves, remembered, "Congress met in extra session, at Blodgett's old shell of a house on 7th street (where the General Post Office now stands). It was three stories high, and had been used for a theatre, a tavern, an Irish boarding-house, etc. ; but both Houses of Congress managed to get along, notwithstanding it had to accommodate the Patent-office, City and General Post-office, committee- rooms, and what was left of the Congressional Library, at the same time. ... The next summer Mr. John Law, a large property holder about the Capitol, fearing it would not be re-built, got up a subscription and built a large brick building…and offered it to Congress for their use, till the Capitol should be re-built. This coaxed them back, though strong efforts were made to move the seat of government North; but the Southern members kept it here."

Not surprisingly, those most grieved by the loss of the first Capitol were the men who had worked the hardest to build it. In 1816, Latrobe detailed the damage the fire had caused: "The South Wing- of the Capitol remains internally in the state in which it was left at the close of the year 1815, excepting in as far as the suggestions of the committee of the House of

Representatives . . . have been so far executed as to prepare the south windows of their hall for an access to a platform along the south front. Externally all the injury which was done to the windows and doors by the fire, has been repaired…. The Hall of Representatives was so ruined that, although the columns and the vaults still stood, it was inevitably necessary to take them down, so as to clear the whole area of the principal story of the former work."

As Latrobe mentioned, the North Wing was in even worse shape than the South Wing. "The North Wing of the Capitol was left after the fire in a much more ruinous state than the South Wing. The whole of the interior of the west side having been constructed of timber, and the old shingle roof still remaining over the greatest part of the wing, an intensity of heat was produced which burnt the walls most exposed to it, and, being driven by the wind into the Senate chamber, burnt the marble columns to lime, cracked everything that was of free-stone, and, finding vent through the windows and up the private stairs, damaged the exterior of the wing very materially. Great efforts were made to destroy the court room, which was built with uncommon solidity, by collecting into it, and setting fire to, the furniture of the adjacent rooms. By this means the columns were cracked exceedingly; but it still stood, and the vault was uninjured. It was, however, very slenderly supported and its condition dangerous. Of the Senate chamber no parts were injured but such as were of marble or free-stone. The vault was entire, and required no repair whatever. The great staircase was much defaced, but might have been reinstated without being taken down. In this state the North Wing was found when the work on the Capitol was commenced in 1815."

One of the problems facing those working to rebuild the Capitol was the dearth of building materials in the area. Latrobe explained, "For the columns, and for various other parts of the House of Representatives, no free-stone that could be at all admitted has been discovered. Other resources were therefore sought after. A stone hitherto considered only as in encumbrance to agriculture, which exists in inexhaustible quantity at the foot of the most south easterly range of our Atlantic mountains, . . . certainly from the Roanoke to the Schuylkill, and which the present surveyor of the Capitol, and probably others, had many years ago discovered to be very hard but beautiful marble — was examined, and, has been proved to answer every expectation that was formed, not only of its beauty, but of its capacity to furnish columns of any length, and to be applicable to any purpose to which colored marble can be applied. The present commissioner of the public buildings has, therefore, entered into a contract for all the columns, and progress has been made in quarrying them. They may be produced each of a single block. . . . The quarries are situated in Loudon County, Virginia, and Montgomery County, Maryland."

As difficult as it may be to imagine, there were certain advantages to the Capitol having been burned so soon after its completion, most notably the fact that the original plans were still available for review. This obviously helped those rebuilding the structure, who could refer to the plans to determine where things should go. Latrobe continued, "The original document having escaped destruction, the work was begun in conformity thereto, and some progress made in the construction of the offices of the judiciary and of the library, when a very important and extensive improvement of the apartments of Senate was suggested by the honorable body, and ordered by the President to be carried into execution. In pursuance of this order, it was necessary to take down the vaults which had been constructed on the west side of the house and to raise them to the level of the principal floor. This alteration was the only one which affected the work carried up in the year 1815. It was affected in the months of May and June. The ruinous state of the building further required that the dome of the central vestibule, the colonnade, and all the vaulting of the court room, and the dome of the great stairs, with all the walls as far as they were injured, should be taken down. The enlargement of the Senate chamber required that the great dome of that apartment and its semi-circular wall be entirely removed, and that the arches and walls of the two committee rooms, and the lobby adjoining the chamber, should also be demolished. All this was promptly accomplished, and the new apartments carried up with all the speed which was consistent with solidity ; so that all the committee rooms on the floor of the Senate are completely constructed and vaulted, and the wall of the Senate chamber itself has advanced to the height of ten feet from the floor. The new vault of the court room, much more extensive than the former, is also completed. All the new work is so constructed as in no part whatever to bear on the old walls, but to serve as a support to them ; and the whole is so bound and connected together as to render the building much more strong and durable than it was before the conflagration."

Though the builders had the original plans, they were not wedded to them, and in fact, some considered the new project an opportunity to make additions to the original building. Ultimately, the most important addition that they made was the construction of a dome at the center of the building. Latrobe observed, "The center of the North Wing demanded light from above; and its symmetry with the South Wing, which could only be lighted by a cupola, demanded a similar construction on the North Wing. Therefore it was almost unavoidable, and certainly it was highly advisable, that the chimneys should be carried up as well as concealed in the piers of the cupola. This had been done before, and, although the cupola was never raised above the dome, its base had existed, and, with the arches that supported it, remained unimpaired by the fire of 1814. ... But, deprived of this support, the object I had to attain was this: To construct over the cavity of the Senate chamber and its wooden dome an arch or other support sufficient to bear the cupola necessary to light the center of the house, and also to carry six-teen or eighteen chimneys concealed in the cupola, and, at the same time, to produce a handsome effect in looking up from the vestibule of the Senate, from which the whole construction would be seen. And I believe that I perfectly attained this object in all its parts, provided the arch had been made to stand."

By the time he wrote the above report, Latrobe had resigned from working on the restoration and been replaced by George Bulfinch, who would go on to complete the project. At first, it looked as if all was well with the project; not long after taking over, Bulfinch wrote, "When I entered upon the duties of my office as architect of the Capitol, and examined the state of the building, I found that a large arch had been built above the third story of the North Wing, which was intended to support the stone cupola or lantern on the center of the dome. I was pleased with the ingenuity and boldness of the design by which it was intended that a great number of chimneys should be carried upon this arch, and rise in the piers of the cupola between its windows."

Bulfinch

Unfortunately, Bulfinch soon learned there were several issues: "By the 23d of April the chimney flues were all brought into their position on the crown of the arch, when the master workman thought it would be proper to loosen the centers, that the arch might be proved and take its bearings before the stone cupola should be built. On loosening the center, it was found that the crown of the arch settled with it, and that the stones around the circular opening had moved in a few minutes so far as that the opening was four inches larger in one direction than in the other; the joints appearing violently compressed in some parts, and open on the others. The workmen left it in alarm and considered it very hazardous."

Eventually, Bulfinch not only came up with a solution to the problem but also earned himself a permanent place in the history of the building for his work on the dome. "I soon came to the determination that the arch could not bear the weight of the flues and stone cupola, estimated at 200 tons more than it was already charged with; and, after inspecting the foundation resolved to build a cone of brick from the bottom of the dome to the circular opening above, for the purpose of strengthening the arch and supporting the cupola. The great arch in the roof of the North Wing is 40 feet in span from north to south, and 30 ft. wide from east to west, and rises in a semi-circle ; it is intended to support a stone cupola 22 ft. in diameter, with 6 windows in its circumference, and as many piers between them, in which 18 chimney flues are to be carried up from the different apartments of the building. A circular opening is made in the crown of the arch 15 ft. wide (the inner diameter of the cupola), to convey light to the interior, and particularly to the vestibule of the Senate chamber. One cause of the failure of this arch arises from the circumstance that the circular opening is not in the center.... On taking down the centering which opened the soffit or under side of the arch to view, another cause of weakness appeared ; the arch, which is two bricks thick, is ornamented with large caissons or coffers of three feet square, sunk in the depth of one brick, or half its thickness ; these destroy the bond and connection of the work. ... It would be dangerous to trust the arch to bear the weight."

A few weeks later, Bulfinch was able to inform Congress, "A cone of brick has been made under the opening of the arch ; the chimney flues are now brought into their right position, and carried up to the top of the dome roof. The work appears fair and substantial, and capable of sustaining the stone lantern which will now immediately be built upon it."

With the dome safely underway, Bulfinch was able to turn his attention to the devastated North Wing. In November 1818, he wrote, "The stone masons have built, on the outside, the entire balustrade of the east and west sides, and the attic of the north front, and the stone cupola over the dome. Inside, they have laid the marble stairs leading to the principal floor, completed the colonnade of the vestibule and part of the gallery of the Senate chamber. The roof has been covered with copper; the apartments and passages of the upper story are plastered and paved; and the doors, shutters, and other carpenter's work will be finished in a few days. The court room is proceeding in a state of preparation for the use of the court in December. The ceiling of the Senate chamber is rough plastered.... The rich and costly colonnade and gallery of the Senate chamber...is to be wholly of marble.... The columns of Potomac marble of the Representatives room have been prepared and set in their places; the stone entablature, with which they are crowned, and the brick arches connecting them with the walls, are built; the stone enclosure forming the breast of the gallery is nearly complete; the ribs of the dome ceiling are raised and secured ; the outer roof is now raising and will be covered in a fortnight, and the balustrade is nearly entire."

An 1848 daguerreotype of the Capitol

Chapter 5: Four Historical Paintings

"The four historical paintings which adorn the larger panels on the western walls of the rotunda are the work of John Trumbull, a son of Jonathan Trumbull, Revolutionary Governor of Connecticut. They represent vital scenes connected with the War for Independence, in which the artist himself participated. ... In 1817, after spending nearly two years in trying to awaken the sympathies of his government in behalf of American art, Trumbull secured from Congress a resolution, approved February 6th, authorizing the President to employ him to execute four paintings commemorative of the most important events of the American Revolution, to placed, when finished, in the Capitol. This was effected through the influence of the artist's many friends and the interest awakened by the studies which he exhibited for some time in the Hall of Representatives. A spirited debate, which is reported as having been 'interesting, amusing and instructive,' occurred at the third reading upon the question of the passage of the resolution." – George Cochrane Hazelton, *The National Capitol: Its Architecture, Art and History*

With the rotunda completed, Congress decided to commission some paintings to adorn its center hall, and over the next several decades, a total of eight large murals would come to grace the building. The first four of these were completed by John Trumbull, but the new Capitol Building quickly proved to be a poor setting for such magnificent works of art. Trumbull's letter detailing how the atmosphere inside the rotunda effected his art work provides significant insight into the conditions in which the early legislators worked. Trumbull wrote to Congress in December 1828, "On the 30th of May last, I received from the Commissioner of the Public

Buildings a copy of the resolution of the honorable the House of Representatives, dated the 26th of May, authorizing him to take the proper measures for securing the paintings in the Rotundo from the effect of dampness, under my direction. I had always regarded the perpetual admission of damp air into the Rotundo from the crypt below, as the great cause of the evil required to be remedied; and, of course, considered the effectual closing of the aperture which had been left in the center of the floor as an indispensable part of remedy. I had communicated my opinions on this subject to the Chairman of the Committee on the Public Buildings, and had been informed that this had been ordered to be done. So soon, therefore, as I received information from the Commissioner that this work was completed, (as well as an alteration in the skylight, which I had suggested,) and that the workmen and encumbrances were removed out of the room, I came on."

Trumbull

The Capitol Crypt

The Rotunda today

Next, Trumbull detailed what had been done to better preserve the art: "All the paintings were taken down, removed from their frames, taken off from the panels over which they are strained, removed to a dry warm room, and there separately and carefully examined. The material which forms the basis of these paintings is a linen cloth, whose strength and texture is very similar to that used in the top gallant-sails of a ship of war. The substances employed in forming a proper surface for the artist, together with the colors, oils, &c. employed by him in his work, form a sufficient protection for the threads of the canvas on this face, but the back remains bare, and, of course, exposed to the deleterious influence of damp air. The effect of this is first seen in the form of mildew; it was this which I dreaded ; and the examination showed that mildew was already commenced, and to an extent which rendered it manifest that the continuance of the same exposure, which they had hitherto undergone, for a very few years longer, would have accomplished the complete decomposition or rotting of the canvas, and the consequent destruction of the paintings. The first thing to be done was to dry the canvas perfectly, which was accomplished by laying down each picture successively on its face, upon a clean dry carpet, and exposing the back to the influence of the warmth of a dry and well aired room. The next thing was to devise and apply some substance which would act permanently as a preservative against future possible exposure. ... Common beeswax was melted over the fire with an equal quantity (in bulk) of oil of turpentine ; and this mixture, by the help of large brushes, was applied hot to the back of each cloth, and was afterwards rubbed in with hot irons, until the cloths were perfectly saturated."

With the canvases protected, Trumbull went on to describe what was done to prevent the dampness from affecting them again. "In the meantime, the niches in the solid wall, in which the paintings are placed, were carefully plastered with hydraulic cement, to prevent any possible exudation of moisture from the wall ; and as there is a space from 2 to 8 inches deep between the surface of the wall and the back of the panels on which the cloths are strained, I caused small openings to be cut into the wall, above and under the edge of the frames, and communicating with those vacant spaces, for the purpose of admitting the air of the room behind the paintings, and thus keeping up a constant ventilation, by means of which the same temperature of air will be maintained at the back of the paintings as on their face."

Once they were thoroughly dry, the canvases were again stretched and hung. Trumbull remarked, "The cloths were finally strained upon panels, for the purpose of guarding against injury from careless or intentional blows of sticks, canes, &c., or children's' missiles. These panels are perforated with many holes, to admit the air freely to the back of the cloths; and being perfectly dried, were carefully painted, to prevent the wood from absorbing or transmitting any humidity. The whole were then restored to their places, and finally cleaned with care, and slightly re-varnished. As the accumulation of dust arising from sweeping so large a room, and, what is much worse, the filth of flies, (the most destructive enemies of painting,) if not carefully guarded against, renders necessary the frequent washing and cleaning of the surface of pictures, every repetition of which is injurious, I have directed curtains to be placed, which can be drawn in front of the whole, whenever the room is to be swept, as well as in the recess of the Legislature during the Summer, when flies are most pernicious."

As Trumbull indicates, the nation's politicians were plagued by flies in the summer and by damp conditions year round, but they also had other woes. Trumbull continued, "As nothing is more obvious than the impossibility of keeping a room warm and dry by means of fire, so long as doors are left open for the admission of the external air, I have further directed self-closing baise doors to be prepared and placed, so that they will unavoidably close behind every one who shall either enter or leave the room. When the doors are kept closed, and fires lighted in the furnaces below, to supply warm air, I find the temperature of this vast apartment is easily maintained at about 68 of Fahrenheit; and the simple precaution of closed doors being observed, in addition to the others which I have employed, I entertain no doubt that these paintings are now perfectly and permanently secured against the deleterious effects of dampness."

These problems stemmed in part from the fact that the Capitol was also becoming too small, for as the country grew, so did the number of representatives meeting and working in its hallowed halls. In 1843, the Senate ordered that "the Secretary of War be requested to cause a plan and estimates to be prepared at the Topographical Bureau, or otherwise within his Department, and laid before Congress at its next session, for a room or apartment in the Capitol, or to be added thereto, for the better accommodation of the sittings of the House of Representatives." Nothing happened right away, but on behalf of the Senate Committee on Public Buildings in 1850, Senator Jefferson Davis, who would become President of the Confederacy about a decade later, accepted architect Robert Mills' plans to add additions to the North and South Wings of the existing building and enlarge the dome.

Mills

While the project was approved and financed by the Congress, Mills' plans were replaced by those of T.U. Walter in 1851. On July 4, 1851, the cornerstone for the new additions was laid, and inside the stone was a note written by the famous writer and orator Daniel Webster. The not read, "On the morning of the first day of the seventy-sixth year of the independence of the United States of America, in the city of Washington, being the fourth day of July, 1851, this stone, designated as the corner-stone of the extension of the Capitol, according to a plan approved by the President, in pursuance of an act of Congress, was laid by Millard Fillmore, President of the United States…If, therefore, it shall hereafter be the will of God that this structure shall fall from its base, that its foundations be up-turned, and this deposit brought to the eyes of men, be it known that, on this day, the Union of the United States of America stands firm ; that their constitution still exists unimpaired, and with all its original usefulness and glory, growing every day stronger and stronger in the affections of the great body of the American people, and attracting more and more the admiration of the world. And all here assembled, whether belonging to public or private life, with hearts devoutly thankful to Almighty God, for the preservation of the liberty and happiness of the country, unite in sincere and fervent prayers that this deposit and the wills and arches, the domes and towers, the columns and entablatures, now to be erected over it, may endure forever! God Save the United States of America!"

Webster

Walter

Chapter 6: Great Difficulty

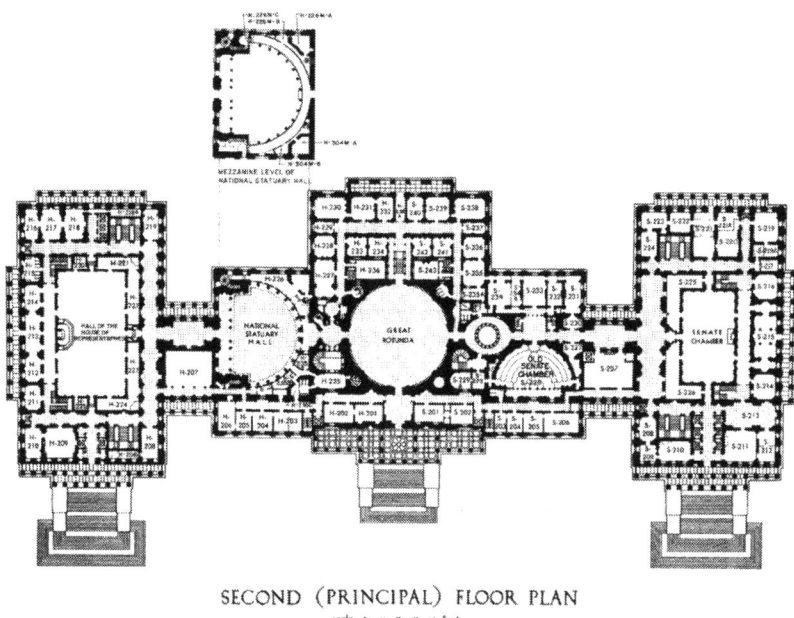

SECOND (PRINCIPAL) FLOOR PLAN
AS OF JUNE, 1997 NORTH →

The floor plan of the current Capitol with the Rotunda and Statuary Hall in the center between the wings for the Senate and House

"Great difficulty was experienced in the building of the foundations, especially at the northwest corner of the Senate wing, where the soil was very sandy. At that point, the walls were sunk forty feet below the surface before final strata could be found. In the fall of 1854, the walls of the House and Senate were up to the ceiling; but they were not covered in with the metallic and glass roofing until 1856. The wings were practically complete in 1861. The east portico of the North Wing was finished in November, 1864. The walls of the beautiful extensions are of white marble from the quarries at Lee, Massachusetts, and are not inharmonious with the walls of the old building, which are of yellowish freestone, painted white. Fifty Corinthian marble columns from quarries at Cockeysville, Maryland, are distributed about the exterior of each new wing and its connecting corridor. The shafts are fluted monoliths, and the capitals and pedestals also are carved of solid slabs of marble. Each column weighs 33 tons, and cost the United States, when in position, $1,550." – George Cochrane Hazelton, *The National Capitol: Its Architecture, Art and History*

George Hazelton wrote in his history on the Capitol about the difficulties presented by the construction process, and they were exacerbated by the fact that the country itself faced great difficulties. As he noted, "The first column was erected on the House wing in November 1860, but the last, which was on the Senate wing, was not raised to its place until 1865. The architraves, entablatures, ornamented pediments, cornices and portico-ceiling-s are composed of massive blocks of marble, in some instances finely carved. Along the west side of each extension run porticoes 105 feet 8 inches in length, projecting 10 feet 6 inches from the wall. Like porticoes extend along the north end of the North Wing and the south end of the South Wing; while double porticoes are formed in each instance to the east. Suitable porte-cocheres beneath the three flights of steps leading to the eastern entrances protect carriage visitors from inclement weather."

A picture of Lincoln's inauguration at the Capitol in 1861

Due to the Civil War, it took more than a decade to complete work on the additions to the Capitol, but when it was finally completed, those who had been part of the project had a right to feel proud. As Hazelton wrote a few decades later, "The style of architecture of the old Capitol, which, from the first, was of the Corinthian order, has been carefully preserved by Walter. Each marble wing is 142 feet 8 inches in length on the east front, by 238 feet 10 inches in depth, exclusive of porticoes and steps. The greatest depth, including the porticoes and steps, is 348 feet 6 inches. Each wing is connected with the old building by a north and south corridor 44 feet in length by 56 feet 8 inches in width, enriched by Corinthian columns similar to those on the wings themselves. These marble extensions have increased the length of the Capitol to 751 feet 4 inches. It covers an area of 153,112 square feet. The official tabulation gives $8,075,299.04 as the net expenditures by the government upon the extensions. ... The House met for the first time in the new Hall of Representatives in the south extension at twelve o'clock, December 16, 1857. The new Senate Chamber was not ready for occupancy for more than a year later, January 4, 1859, when the Senate moved from its old chamber." The Corinthian columns on the East Portico were removed a century later and now stand in the National Arboretum.

Since the new additions made the original dome look paltry, Walters designed a new, much larger dome to replace the original. Hazelton described the new dome: "Great engineering skill was required in the erection of the dome. The walls had to be trussed, bolted, girded and lamped in every conceivable way to hold in position the immense superstructure. Even furnished with the figures, it is scarcely possible for the mind to appreciate its immense weight. Walter calculated its 8,909,200 pounds of cast and wrought iron as giving a pressure of 13,477 pounds to the square foot at the basement floor, and the supporting walls as capable of holding 755,280 pounds to the same area. The pressure upon the walls of the cellar floor, exclusive of the weight of the Goddess of Freedom, is estimated at 51,292,253 pounds. The dome is composed of two shells, one within the other, which expand and contract with the variations in temperature • between these the stairway winds in its ascent. The greatest diameter at the base is 135 feet 5 inches. The cost of the new dome is officially given at $1,047,291.89. The thirty-six columns which surround the lower portion of the exterior represent the thirty-six States in the Union at the time it was designed. The thirteen columns which encircle the lantern above the tholos are emblematic of the thirteen original States. This lantern is 24 feet 4 inches in diameter and 50 feet in height."

The fresco on dome's ceiling depicts the apotheosis of Washington

Matt Wade's picture of the dome's interior with Washington's statue in the foreground

The Goddess of Freedom statue Hazelton referred to was both the literal and figurative crowning touch of the building. It was not created in the United States but in Rome by sculptor Thomas Crawford in 1855, and like so much else to do with the capital, it was plagued by controversy. Crawford wrote to Captain Montgomery Meigs in 1855, "It is quite possible that Mr. Jefferson Davis may, as upon a former occasion, object to the cap of Liberty and the fasces. I can only say in reply that the work is for the people, and they must be addressed in language they understand, and which has become unalterable for the masses. The emblems I allude to can never be replaced by any invention of the artist; all that can be done, is to add to them, as I have done, by placing the circlet of stars around the cap of liberty: it thus becomes more picturesque, and nothing of its generally understood signification is lost. All arguments, however, must reduce themselves into the question: 'Will the people understand it? I, therefore, hope [Davis] will allow the emblems to 'pass muster.' I have said the statue represents 'armed Liberty.' She rests upon the shield of our country, the triumph of which is made apparent by the wreath held in the same hand which grasps the shield; in her right hand she holds the sheathed sword, to show the fight is over for the present, but ready for use whenever required. The stars upon her brow indicate her heavenly origin; her position upon the globe represents her protection of the

American world — the justice of whose cause is made apparent by the emblems supporting it."

Andreas Praefcke's picture of the Statue of Freedom

Crawford

The issue of the statue's head gear continued to be a bone of contention, primarily because of the tensions in the country at that time over the issue of slavery. Davis wrote in January 1856, "The second photograph of the statue with which it is proposed to crown the dome of the Capitol, impresses me most favorably. Its general grace and power, striking at first view, has grown on me as I studied its details. As to the cap, I can only say, without intending to press the objection formerly made, that it seems to me its history renders it inappropriate to a people who were born free and would not be enslaved. The language of art, like all living tongues, is subject to change ; thus the bundle of rods, if no longer employed to suggest the functions of the Roman Lictor, may lose the symbolic character derived therefrom, and be confined to the single signification drawn from its other source — the fable teaching the instructive lesson that in union there is strength. But the liberty cap has an established origin in its use, as the badge of the freed slave; and though it should have another emblematic meaning to-day, a recurrence to that origin may give to it in the future the same popular acceptation which it had in the past. Why should not armed Liberty wear a helmet? Her conflict being over, her cause triumphant, as shown by the other emblems of the statue, the visor would be up so as to permit, as in the photograph, the display of a circle of stars, expressive of endless existence and of heavenly birth."

Walter decided it was best to go along with Davis' requests, and in March 1856, Crawford wrote to Meigs again: "I read with much pleasure the letter of the honorable Secretary [of War, Davis], and his remarks have induced me to dispense with the ' cap ' and put in its place a helmet, the crest of which is composed of an eagle's head and a bold arrangement of feathers, suggested by the costume of our Indian tribes."

Davis

Meigs

Chapter 7: An Unfinished Appearance

"Even after the erection of the grand marble wings and the elevation of the dome, the Capitol, except on the eastern front, had an unfinished appearance despite the sodded embankment which formed the old terrace, especially devised by Bulfinch. ... The present terrace, which greatly enhances the beauty of the building, was designed by, and constructed under the direction of, Edward Clark, the present distinguished architect of the Capitol. Clark was first initiated into office as the assistant of Walter, the architect of the extensions, and assumed his present position after the completion of the marble wings and the new dome, upon which his best energies and talents had been displayed in seconding Walter's plans." – George Cochrane Hazelton, *The National Capitol: Its Architecture, Art and History*

In addition to the building itself, much was done during this time to make the landscaping around the Capitol more appealing. One man observed in 1842, "Proceeding through the western entrance of the Capitol you reach a spacious terrace, paved with Seneca freestone, and extending in a very beautiful sweep, from north to south. Beneath this terrace,' which is below the level of the east front, is a range of casemate arches, forming depositories for the wood and coal annually consumed in the building. The terrace is faced with a grass bank or glacis, and accessible by two flights of stone steps on either side of the open arches leading to the basement story of the Capitol. Under the middle of these is a handsome marble fountain, from which the water, brought through pipes from springs about two miles north of the Capitol, falls into a beautiful basin of white marble, and thence flows into a reservoir cased with stone, and in which has been erected a monument to the memory of young naval officers, Somers, Wadsworth, Israel, Decatur, Dorsey, and Caldwell, who gallantly perished off Tripoli, in 1804. It is a Doric pillar, with emblematic embellishments, etc., crowned with an eagle in the act of flying. The column ornamented with the prows of Turkish vessels, rests on a base, on one side of which is sculptured in basso relievo a view of Tripoli and its fortresses in the distance, the Mediterranean and American fleet in the foreground. The whole monument is of Italian marble, and its sub-base of American marble, found near Baltimore."

An aerial photo of Capitol Hill

In addition to the statues, the design's layout provided for beautiful paths through which those visiting the Capitol could roam: "Further west is another fall or glacis, with stone steps, from the bottom of which three fine walks, paved with granite, lead to the principal western gates, one in the center, one opening into the Maryland, and the other into Pennsylvania Avenue. On each side of the center gateway are porters' lodges, which, with the stone piers to the gates, are constructed in the same style as the basement of the building. The public grounds around the Capitol are enclosed by an iron palisade or railing, bordered with a belt of forest and ornamental trees, shrubs, and flowers, and laid out into walks neatly graveled, and also planted with fine trees. On each side of the center walk are two small jets d'eau, supplied with water from the reservoir above. A brick pavement extends along the wall, on the outside, upwards of a mile in length, and the square or public grounds form, in fine weather, one of the most beautiful promenades in this country."

Over the next several decades, more statues were added to the area around the Capitol, and Hazelton briefly described the changes that had taken place during his lifetime: "The present terrace, which greatly enhances the beauty of the building, was designed by, and constructed under the direction of, Edward Clark, the present distinguished architect of the Capitol. Clark was first initiated into office as the assistant of Walter, the architect of the extensions, and assumed his present position after the completion of the marble wings and the new dome, upon which his best energies and talents had been displayed in seconding Walter's plans. The approaches were begun in 1882; the terrace itself was not commenced until two years later, nor finished until 1891, this grand esplanade, which extends along the entire north, south and west fronts of the Capitol, is built principally of Vermont marble. The large interior space secured to the building by means of this addition is occupied by electric plants and the furnaces and engines which heat the building, and by committee rooms and those devoted to the use of the custodian of art. The total cost of the terrace to the government has been about $750,000. The cost of the Capitol up to June 30, 1883, is estimated at $515,599,656, of which $703,455.80 is officially given as the cost of repairs upon the building from March 2, 1827, to March 3, 1875."

By 1897, Hazelton was able to assert, "This terrace is the last touch upon the Capitol. The great pile today, although designed piece by piece under the direction of various architects, has none of the patchwork appearance common to so many of the great buildings of the world. From any one of the magnificent views to be had of the imposing structure, it presents the symmetry, unity and classic grace of a building designed and executed by one master mind. It has grown as the nation has grown. The cornerstone was laid by Washington in 1793; the terrace was finished nearly a hundred years later, in 1891; and yet the Capitol will never be complete while the nation lasts. The impress of each succeeding generation will be found upon its walls, marking the intellectual, artistic and governmental advancement of the age. The great pile is national, American, human. On its walls is written the nation's history. Its corridors resound to the footsteps of her living heroes and sages; its every stone echoes the departed voices of her greatest dead."

The Senate Chamber in the 1870s

A picture of restoration work being done on the dome in 2014

Bibliography

Allen, William C. (2001). *History of the United States Capitol – A Chronicle of Design, Construction, and Politics*. Government Printing Office.

Frary, Ihna Thayer (1969). *They Built the Capitol*. Ayer Publishing.

Hazelton, George Cochrane (1907). *The National Capitol*. J. F. Taylor & Co.

Made in the USA
Las Vegas, NV
26 November 2021